TopReaders

Weather Watching

Denise Ryan

Contents

Weather Engine................................4

World Climate................................6

Seasons................................8

Clouds................................10

Wind................................12

Rain and Snow................................14

Ice and Frost................................16

Lightning................................18

Heavenly Colors................................20

Weather Watching................................22

Reporting Weather................................24

Measuring Weather................................26

Natural Clues................................28

Quiz................................30

Glossary................................31

Index................................32

What is weather? How do we know when it is going to rain? Let's find out.

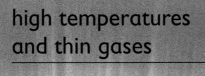

high temperatures
and thin gases

colder
layer

dry,
warm air

Most weather
happens here.

Earth's surface

Key

■ Sunlight is hot
  at the equator.

□ Sunlight is not as
  hot near the North
  and South poles.

Weather Engine

The Sun controls all the weather on
Earth. Heat from the Sun helps clouds
to form and rain to fall.

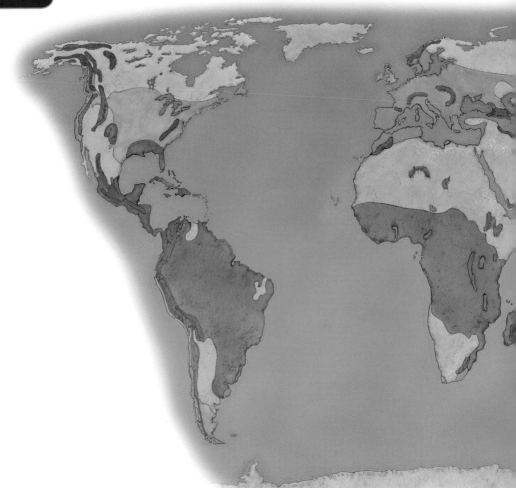

World Climate

The weather that a place normally has is called its climate. Different places can have climates that are hot, cold, or mild.

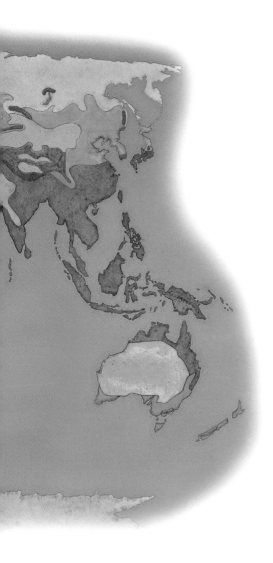

☐ polar

■ mountain

☐ temperate

■ tropical

☐ desert

The map above shows different climate zones. Can you see where the deserts are?

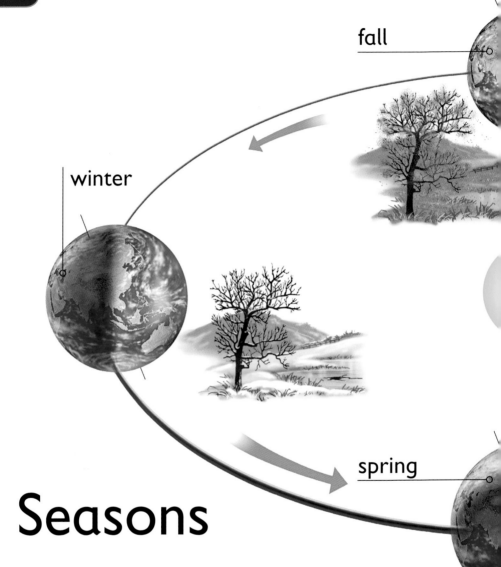

fall

winter

spring

Seasons

Seasons occur because Earth is on a tilt as it moves around the Sun. This gives us four seasons each year— spring, summer, fall, and winter.

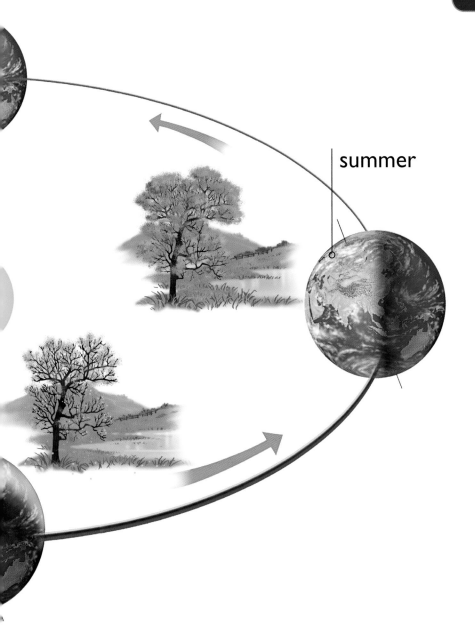

summer

It is warmest in summer and coldest in winter. In fall, the leaves drop off the trees. But in spring they grow back again.

Clouds

Clouds are groups of tiny droplets of water. The droplets are so small and light that they float in the air.

Clouds often appear white. When they hold more water, they appear darker.

Clouds move with the wind.

Wind

Wind is moving air.
Air moves because the
Sun heats Earth's surface
unevenly. The warm air
rises and cool air falls.

cool air falling
over water

cool wind

When warm air rises, cool air flows in to take its place.

warm wind

warm air rising
above land

Rain and Snow

Tiny water droplets in clouds join together to form bigger drops. When those drops get too heavy, they fall as rain.

When it is very cold, the water drops change to ice and fall as hail or snow.

When clouds are very thick and gray, it is time to get out your umbrella!

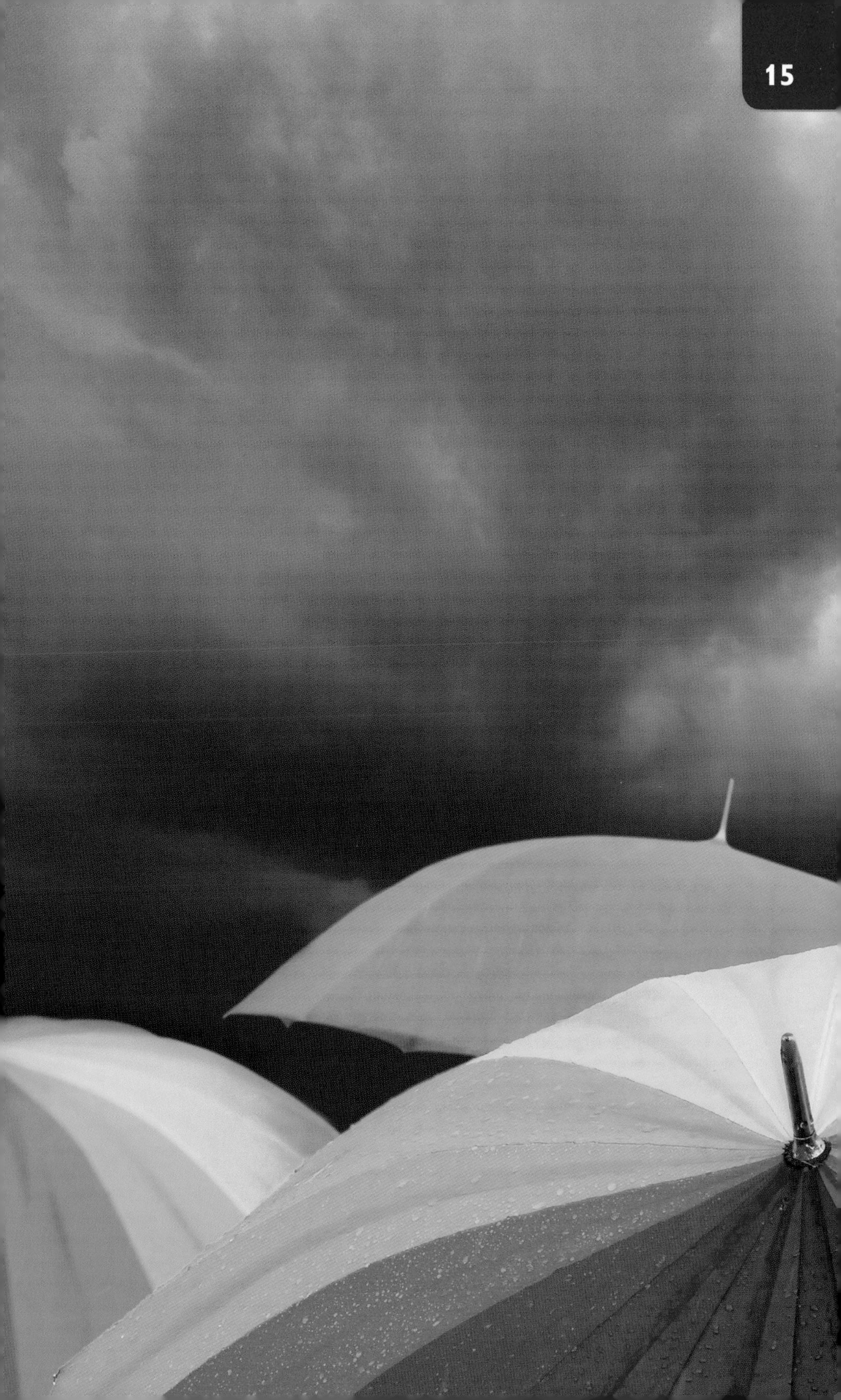

Ice and Frost

These icy white crystals are frost.
Frost forms at night when water
freezes on plants and on the ground.

Frost covers plants and grass.
Ice has formed along the riverbank
and snow is on the trees.

frost on plants

snow on trees

ice on
riverbank

Lightning

Sometimes tiny particles inside clouds can become charged with electricity. Bolts of lightning flash when the electricity builds up.

Lightning usually strikes tall objects, such as trees or buildings.

Heavenly Colors

Rainbows appear when sunlight passes through raindrops. The drops scatter the light in different directions. We see this as the curve of a rainbow.

Sunlight looks white, but it is really made up of different colors.

Key
- 🟥 red
- 🟧 orange
- 🟨 yellow
- 🟩 green
- 🟦 blue
- ⬛ indigo
- 🟪 violet

Weather Watching

Many years ago, scientists learned about temperature , wind, and lightning by sending kites high into the sky.

Long ago, scientists flew kites to measure the air's temperature high above the ground.

Reporting Weather

Today, satellites send weather information to scientists. This helps them report on the weather and forecast hurricanes and tornadoes.

Weather satellites in space send back pictures to Earth.

Measuring Weather

You can measure the weather at home. Use a rain gauge to see how much rain falls every day.

rain gauge

You can use a
thermometer
to measure how hot
or cold it is outside.
Put it behind a
screen to protect it
from direct sunlight.

weather vane

thermometer

screen

Natural Clues

Long before people had weather forecasts, they used clues from nature to tell them what to expect.

People believed these clues meant it was going to rain.

guinea fowl nesting

dragonflies hovering

cats washing

bees buzzing

morning glories
opening

donkey
nodding

pine cones
opening

grasshoppers
chirping

People believed these clues meant
it was going to be fine and warm.

Quiz

Can you match each item with its name?

lightning   clouds

rainbow   rain gauge

Glossary

electricity: a form of energy. It can make small lighbulbs, as well as big trains, work.

forecast: to predict

gauge: an instrument to measure something

nature: everything on Earth except those things made by humans

satellites: machines that are launched into space and that move around Earth

scientists: people who study nature

temperature: a measure of the degree of hotness or coldness

thermometer: an instrument to measure temperature

tilt: a sloping position

Index

climate	6, 7
clouds	5, 10, 11, 14, 18
Earth	4, 5, 8, 12, 25
frost	16
hail	14
hurricanes	25
ice	14, 16, 17
lightning	18, 19, 22
rain	3, 5, 14, 26
seasons	8
snow	14, 16, 17
Sun	5, 8, 12
temperature	22
water	10, 11, 14, 16